On the Move

Contents

Features

Turn to page 4 to read about a scientist who made an important discovery about energy.

People use electricity constantly in their daily lives so what happens when the electricity fails? Read page 7 and think about it.

How do people lift very heavy weights? One way is to use a system of pulleys. See for yourself by following the instructions in **Make Your Own Block and Tackle** on page 22.

How does a car engine work? Have a look at **The Internal Combustion Engine** on page 25 to find out.

Does gravity exist inside a spacecraft?

Visit www.infosteps.co.uk
for more about **PHYSICS.**

Why Things Move

When a ball is thrown into the air it always comes back down. When the wind blows it rustles the leaves on the trees. When you use a straw to drink your soft drink the liquid travels to your mouth easily. These things might seem very obvious, but they all have one important factor in common—they all use **force**. Without force the ball would stay in the air, the leaves would remain still and the straw wouldn't work.

While these forces are different they all need **energy** to work. Every time something moves it is a result of energy being used. The science of the properties of matter and energy is called physics.

PROFILE

James Prescott Joule (1818—1889)

James Prescott Joule was an English **physicist** who made the discovery that heat is energy. A unit of energy, the joule, is named after him.

Everything that happens in the physical world involves force. When things move, stop or change direction forces are acting on them.

Providing Energy

Forms of Energy

Without energy absolutely nothing would happen and no life would exist on Earth. Energy is all around us. It cannot be created or destroyed. When people say that energy is being lost it isn't exactly true. Energy can never be lost—only changed in some way. This fact is the first law of **thermodynamics**, or the principle of the conservation of energy.

Nuclear Fission

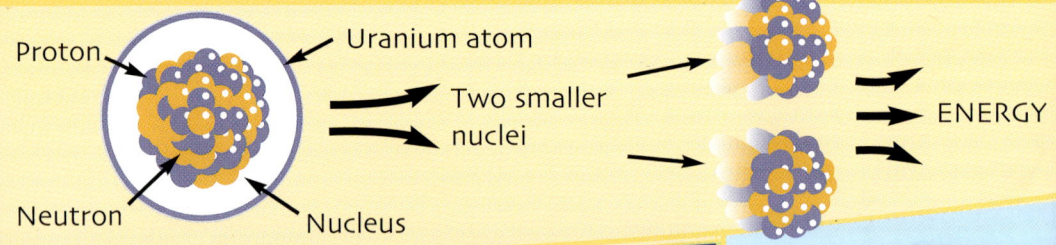

Proton
Uranium atom
Two smaller nuclei
ENERGY
Neutron
Nucleus

Nuclear fission is used to produce electricity in many countries around the world. Nuclear fission is the process of splitting the core, or nucleus, of a uranium **atom**. Splitting an atom releases a huge amount of energy.

Many forms of energy can be generated in a variety of ways. Electrical energy can be produced using the force of the wind or running water, or by burning coal, oil or other fuels. Electricity is also produced by nuclear power plants.

Life for most people has become almost totally reliant on electricity. Millions of people had to do without it when seven US states, including the city of New York and parts of Canada lost electricity in a blackout on August 17, 2003. Public transportation systems, lights, air-conditioning and appliances didn't work for nearly 29 hours.

WHAT'S YOUR OPINION?

I think we're too dependent on electricity. When there's a power failure, nothing works! No backup system is foolproof. We have to be more prepared in the future.

The New York City skyline during the August, 2003 blackout

Energy Transformation

Before energy can be of much use it needs to be transformed. This means that one type of energy becomes another type of energy. Energy transformations are taking place around us all the time. Electrical energy is converted to light energy when we turn on a light. Chemical energy is converted to light and heat energy when we light a fire.

Some energy transformations involve many changes. For example, a wind turbine changes wind energy to mechanical energy. This mechanical energy can power a generator which produces electrical energy. That electrical energy can then be transformed into sound energy when we switch on our radios.

Two Examples of Energy Transformations

Source	Device	Change
Chemical energy	burning candle	light and heat energy
Electrical energy	speaker	sound energy

Some energy transformations can damage the environment. Lakes and rivers can be affected when water is used to create hydroelectricity. Burning fossil fuels causes air pollution. Fossil fuels are also in limited supply.

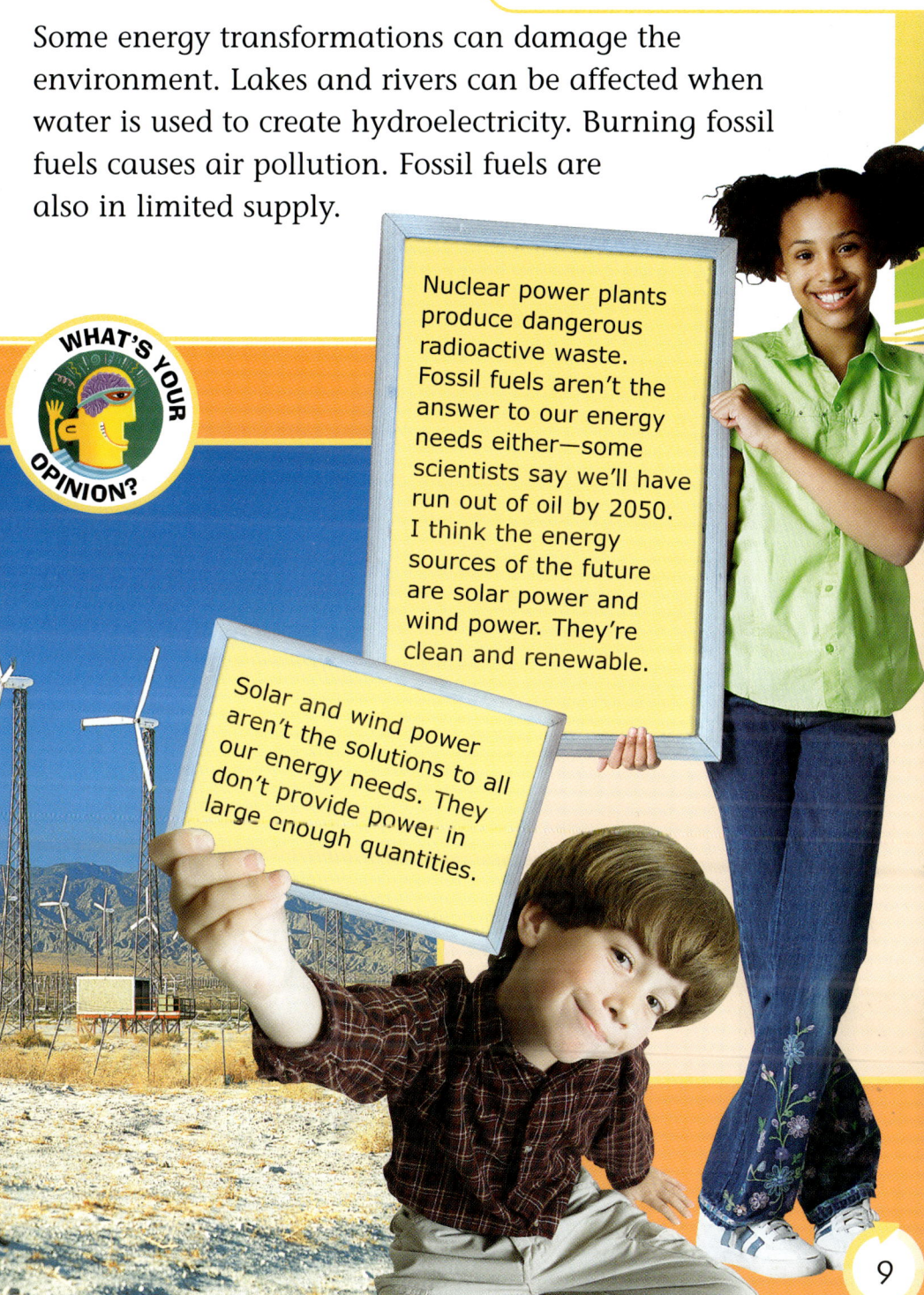

WHAT'S YOUR OPINION?

Nuclear power plants produce dangerous radioactive waste. Fossil fuels aren't the answer to our energy needs either—some scientists say we'll have run out of oil by 2050. I think the energy sources of the future are solar power and wind power. They're clean and renewable.

Solar and wind power aren't the solutions to all our energy needs. They don't provide power in large enough quantities.

Potential and Kinetic Energy

One of the most important types of energy transformation is from potential to **kinetic** energy. Potential energy is the energ that is stored in an object. Kinetic energy is the energy of motion. A rubber band gains potential energy when it is stretched. When it is released the potential energy is transformed into kinetic energy.

Kinetic energy is important in creating other forms of energy. Water at the top of a waterfall has potential energy. As it drop down it is converted to kinetic energy. This kinetic energy can then be used to turn a turbine and produce electrical energy.

At the highest part of a jump a skateboarder has maximum potential energy. As the skateboarder descends this becomes kinetic energy.

When a wound-up yo-yo is held in your hand at a height it has maximum potential energy. As it falls the potential energy is gradually converted to kinetic energy. When the yo-yo reaches the bottom of its string it has no potential energy and maximum kinetic energy.

TRY THIS!

Energy Experiment

You will need:

• a 7.5 x 12.5 cm card

• scissors

• a rubber band

1. Fold the card in half.
2. Cut two slits about 2.5 cm deep and 2.5 cm apart on each side of the card.
3. Loop the rubber band through the four slits.

4. Flatten out the card. Then let go. What happens?*

*The potential energy in the rubber band is released and becomes the kinetic energy that moves the card.

Consuming Energy

Whether we are running a marathon or quietly reading a book we are using energy. The more active we are the more energy we use. Our energy comes from the food we eat. Chemical energy is stored in food. Our bodies convert this energy into other forms when we eat.

When we run our bodies transform the chemical energy of food into kinetic energy.

Chemical energy is transformed into electrical energy that our nervous system uses to transmit information from one cell to another, telling muscles to act. Muscles also transform chemical energy into kinetic energy allowing us to move.

Much of the energy we get from food is turned into heat to keep us warm. A healthy balanced diet is essential to provide us with the energy we need.

Photosynthesis

Plants get their energy directly from the sun. They transform the sun's **radiant** energy into food in a process called photosynthesis. People get their energy indirectly from the sun by eating plants or by eating animals that have eaten plants.

Radiant energy

Oxygen

Carbon dioxide

Glucose, sucrose and other carbohydrates are made in the tree's leaves.

Water

13

Athletes often eat more of certain types of food as they use more energy. Running, swimming, cycling and other sports require strong muscles so athletes eat a lot of carbohydrates such as those found in potatoes, bread, rice and pasta. Carbohydrates are the form of plant energy most easily converted by people into the energy they need.

The more you exercise the stronger your muscles become. During exercise the body takes in more oxygen and the heart pumps more blood. You don't need to be a world-class athlete to benefit from exercise. Regular exercise helps every person become fitter, feel better and enjoy life more.

You might think that more energy is used to ride a bike than to travel in a car, but in fact travelling a kilometre by car uses much more energy than travelling a kilometre by bicycle. The fuel used by cars is not renewable unlike the fuel used by people—food!

Calories and kilojoules are the units used to measure the energy value of food. One calorie equals 4.2 kilojoules.

Each 100 kilojoules you consume will give you enough energy to:

- jog for two minutes
- cycle for three minutes
- walk quickly for five minutes
- sleep for half an hour!

Forces of Nature

Gravity

All forces use energy either to pull or push an object. Some forces, including the force used when pushing a swing, are easier to understand than others. You can see a person using energy to push the swing.

Other forces are not as easy to see. The swing is either pushed or pulled in one direction, but what force pulls it back in the other direction? This force is called gravity. The force of gravity pulls everything towards the centre of Earth. Gravity is what keeps us all from floating into space!

All large bodies such as planets, moons and stars have gravity, though each planet's gravity is different. Scientists use complex machines such as the gravity wave machine (shown left) to measure gravity on other planets.

The force of hot air rising in one direction overcomes the gravity pulling in the other direction, allowing hot-air balloons to float. Pilots control hot-air balloons by letting more or less hot air into the balloon. Hot air rises and cold air sinks so the balloon descends when the pilot allows the air to cool.

Gravity

Air pressure

G-WHAT

Friction

When the surfaces of objects are rubbed together a force called friction occurs. Friction is one of the reasons (gravity is another) that we are able to slow down when we are running. Friction is also the reason it takes a lot of energy to speed up. When surfaces are rough there is more friction. Smooth surfaces such as ice have less friction so activities such as skating require less energy. Friction can be reduced by using a **lubricant** between surfaces.

Dolphins slip easily through water because their **streamlined** shape minimizes the effect of friction. Friction causes **drag** which slows objects down. To reduce drag objects such as yachts, planes and racing cars are streamlined too.

Friction and the lack of friction help us in different ways. The oil on a bicycle chain helps reduce friction so you use less energy to pedal. When you need to brake quickly your brakes increase friction.

Friction also produces heat. That is why rubbing two sticks together is an ancient way of starting a fire. The sticks become hot and ignite kindling.

In a tug-of-war friction helps you hold the rope tightly. Your hands are smooth, but the rope is rough.

Combined Forces

Most objects have more than one force acting on them. An aeroplane, for example, has several forces. Gravity pulls it downwards while air beneath the wings lifts it up. **Air resistance** produces a slowing force, or drag, and the engine provides a forward thrust. The combined effect of all these forces is called the **resultant**. The pilot must work out a balance of these forces in order to fly or land the plane.

Air resistance acts as a slowing force.

The force of **buoyancy** keeps boats from sinking, but boats are also affected by the forces of wind and water.

In many situations forces cancel each other out and the resultant is zero. This means that no overall force is acting and the object is either still or moving at a constant speed. When a pony is pulling a cart at a steady speed, for example, the pulling force of the pony is exactly balanced by the frictional drag between the road and the wheels of the cart. An object whose speed is not changing is said to be in a state of **equilibrium**.

Forces Acting on an Aeroplane

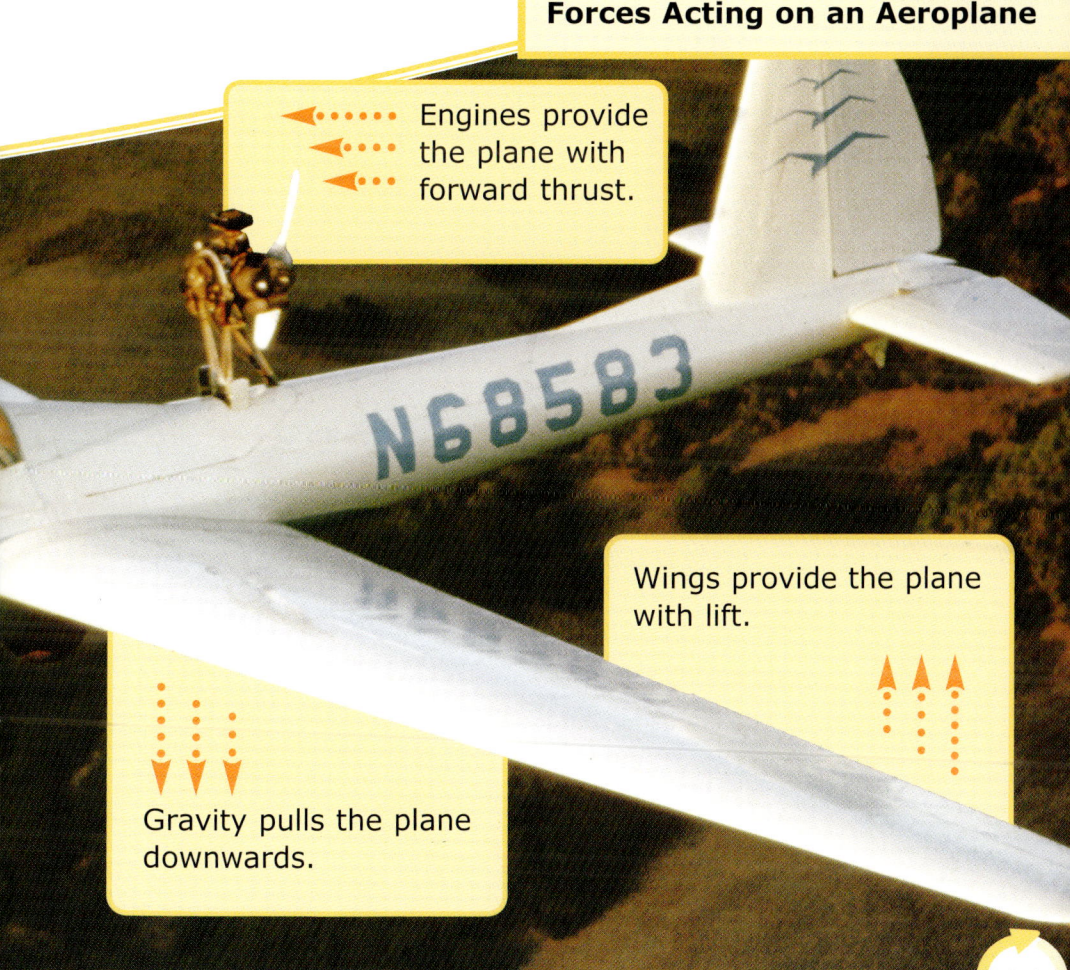

Engines provide the plane with forward thrust.

Wings provide the plane with lift.

Gravity pulls the plane downwards.

Marvellous Machines

Simple Machines

When the word *work* is used in science it doesn't refer to a job. Work means using a force. We are doing work whenever we use our muscles to lift or move something.

We have discovered or invented simple machines to do much of our work for us. These machines use some of the forces found in nature to perform work. Simple machines can be found being used in nearly everything we do. These simple machines include levers, wheels, **pulleys**, ramps, wedges and screws.

TRY THIS!

Make Your Own Block and Tackle

Pulleys used together are called a block and tackle.

Step 1
Thread a length of string through the holes in two empty cotton reels placed end to end. Tie the ends of the string to a hook.

Step 2
Thread a second length of string through the holes in another two cotton reels, and tie the ends of the string to the handle of a small bucket or object.

Step 3
Tie a third length of string to the hook. Thread it around the cotton reels, as shown in the illustration. The top spools are the block and the lower spools are the tackle. Pulling the string lifts the bucket.

Levers

Levers help us move weights more easily. They distribute the load to help overcome the force of gravity. A wheelbarrow is a simple machine that uses a lever.

Pulleys

Pulleys change the direction of a force. This helps to overcome gravity. A pulley makes it much easier to pull up a heavy bucket of water from a well.

Wheels

Wheels help us move around more easily. Because only a small part of a wheel is in contact with a surface at any time, it can overcome the slowing force of friction.

Space Force

What happens to the force of gravity in space? How does work change when the force of gravity is altered or absent? Since the earliest days of spaceflight scientists have been studying what happens in zero gravity.

Chemicals react differently when there is no gravity. Substances that help in the treatment of diseases such as cancer and diabetes may come one day from experiments in space. Lighter stronger metals and other new materials can be produced more easily in zero gravity. The possibilities are exciting. Who knows what other technologies will be developed as a result of working in zero gravity?

Effects of Zero Gravity

Floating around in zero gravity sounds like fun, but in fact lack of gravity has its problems. In zero gravity the density of bones tends to decrease and muscles, especially in the legs and back, are weakened. Also blood moves from the lower half of the body towards the heart and head.

These events can become problems for astronauts when they return to the full gravity of Earth. Scientists are studying ways to lessen these effects.

Tremendous power is needed to overcome Earth's gravity and blast off into space.

Does gravity exist inside a spacecraft?

Visit **www.infosteps.co.uk**
for more about **PHYSICS.**

SITESEEING · SCIENCE & TECHNOLOGY

29

Glossary

air resistance – friction experienced by an object travelling through air

atom – the smallest particle of a chemical element. Everything in the universe is made up of atoms.

buoyancy – the force that causes an object to float or rise when it is pushed down into a liquid

drag – the slowing force of air or liquid on a moving object

energy – the power which allows work to be done

equilibrium – a state in which opposing forces or influences are balanced

force – a power that causes change in movement

kinetic – to do with movement or caused by movement. Kinetic energy is the energy of a moving object.

lubricant – a substance that reduces the effects of friction

physicist – a scientist who studies physics, the science of matter and energy

pulley – a wheel with a groove around its rim. This simple machine is used to lift very heavy weights.

radiant – transmitted by electromagnetic radiation

resultant – the single force that has the same effect as many forces acting on an object

streamlined – shaped so that air or water flows smoothly over its surface when it is moving. Dolphins are very streamlined.

thermodynamics – the study of heat and work

Index

Research Starters

1 Earth and the other eight planets in our solar system orbit the sun. Find out why this happens.

2 For centuries people have been searching for a perpetual-motion machine. Find out what *perpetual motion* means. How close are scientists to developing such a device?

3 People use many simple and complex machines to help them do their work. Research to make lists of important simple and complex machines. Which do you consider to be the most important machine ever invented? Give the reasons for your choice.

4 What kinds of fuels are renewable and which of these are being developed now? Why is it important to use renewable fuels whenever possible?